Moray & Nairn Family History Society

The Parishes of Nairnshire
Deaths & Places of Burial
1855-1860

Ardclach & Cawdor

Compiled by
Janet M Bishop & Kenneth A M Nisbet

Copyright © 2009 Moray & Nairn Family History Society

ISBN 978-0-9561937-2-8

First published April 2009

Published by
J & B Bishop for
Moray & Nairn Family History Society

Printed by
Parchments of Oxford, Crescent Road, Cowley, Oxford

INTRODUCTION

Finding the burial place of ancestors is often difficult, as most families were not able to afford to erect a headstone, and therefore their deaths would not be recorded in a book of monumental inscriptions. The idea for this series of books came from the fact that, in the first 6 years of Statutory Registration in Scotland, death certificates included a column for the recording of the place of burial, which was certified, usually by the undertaker.

Statutory Registration began in Scotland in 1855, and this volume records the burial places of those who died in the parishes of Ardclach and Cawdor, in the years 1855-1860, so that even if there is no headstone, the researcher can still visit the churchyard in which his ancestors are buried.

The following abbreviations are used throughout, with regard to ages:

c	circa (about)
d	day/s
h	hour/s
m	month/s
w	week/s

ACKNOWLEDGEMENTS

Acknowledgements are due to members of Moray & Nairn Family History Society, who assisted in the preparation of this publication, and to the publishers for their help in the layout and production.

CONTENTS

The Parishes of Nairnshire
Deaths & Burial Places
1855-1860

Ardclach Parish

Name/Place of Death	Age	Date/Details	Burial Place
ALEXANDER, Catherine	29	8 June 1860 Single; daughter of Duncan Alexander & Margaret Alexander, ms Reid	Auldearn Churchyard
ALEXANDER, Isabella (Drummore)	83	14 March 1859 Widow; grandmother of William McQueen; daughter of Alexander Rose & Elizabeth Rose, ms Falconer	Auldearn Churchyard
ALLAN, James Barron	8m	18 October 1858 Son of John Allan & Mary Allan, ms Barron	Ardclach Churchyard
ANDERSON, Robert	19	13 May 1860 Single; mason; brother of John Anderson; son of Robert Anderson & Elspeth Anderson, ms Anderson	Auldearn Churchyard
CALDER, Robert	16	23 May 1858 Son of John Calder & Catherine Calder, ms Davidson	Braeven, Cawdor
CALLUM, Donald	25	14 December 1855 Single; son of Alexander Callum & Elspet Callum, ms Callum	Ardclach Churchyard
CALLUM, Elspet	72	14 February 1860 Widow; mother of Alexander Callum; daughter of Alexander Callum & Christina Callum, ms McPherson	Ardclach Churchyard
CAMERON, Alexander	62	13 January 1857 Married; shoemaker; son of John Cameron & Sophia Cameron, ms Mackintosh	Ardclach Churchyard

Name/Place of Death	Age	Date/Details	Burial Place
CAMERON, William	74	28 August 1857 Married; farm servant; father of John Cameron, Tullieglens; son of Ewen Cameron & Catherine Cameron, ms McGrigor	Edinkillie Churchyard
CAMPBELL, Bryan (Balvilie)	81	29 September 1856 Married; crofter; grandfather of James McArthur; son of James Campbell & Margaret Campbell, ms McAndrew	Ardclach Churchyard
CAMPBELL, Jane (Hillhead of Fleenas)	21	10 August 1859 Single; daughter of James Campbell & Janet Campbell, ms Fraser	Ardclach Churchyard
CAMPBELL, Janet (Balville)	78	10 May 1858 Widow; grandmother of James McArthur; daughter of David Tulloch & Margaret Tulloch, ms Rose	Ardclach Churchyard
CLARK, Katharine	83	30 January 1860 Widow; daughter of John Gordon & Isabella Gordon, ms Lawson	Ardclach Churchyard
CLUNAS, Mary	69	26 March 1857 Widow; mother in law of James Clunas; daughter of Duncan Clunas & Catherine Clunas, ms MacKintosh	Auldearn Churchyard
COWPAR, Marjory Meek (Bridge of Ardclach)	14	14 January 1855 Brother of Adam Cowpar; son of Charles Cowpar & Maria Cowpar, ms Johnston	Auldearn Churchyard
CRUICKSHANKS, Donald	53	22 December 1855 Married; father of 8; son of James Cruickshanks; mother's ms Cumming	Ardclach Churchyard

Name/Place of Death	Age	Date/Details	Burial Place
CUMMING, Girzal (Mount)	52	28 March 1858 Married; daughter of Charles Grant & Emilia Grant, ms Cumming	Edinkillie Churchyard
DAVIDSON, male	8d	28 November 1857 Infant son of Eliza Davidson	Ardclach Churchyard
DAVIDSON, David	41	5 February 1858 Single; blind; son of John Davidson & Ann Davidson, ms Campbell	Ardclach Churchyard
DAVIDSON, James	23	23 September 1855 Single; brother of Francis Davidson; son of John Davidson & Jean Davidson, ms Urquhart	Ardclach Churchyard
DAVIDSON, John	84	16 June 1856 Widower; farmer; father of Francis Davidson; son of John Davidson & Ann Davidson, ms Cameron	Ardclach Churchyard
DAVIDSON, Margaret	56	28 June 1860 Single; sister of Alexander Davidson; daughter of John Davidson & Isabella Davidson, ms Rose	Ardclach Churchyard
DAVIDSON, Robert (Brevail)	3m	22 March 1857 Illegitimate son of John Davidson & Jane Ross	Auldearn Churchyard
DINGWALL, Margaret	50	21 February 1855 Wife of Alexander Dingwall; mother of 2; daughter of John Mackintosh & Helen Mackie	Ardclach Churchyard

Name/Place of Death	Age	Date/Details	Burial Place
DONALDSON, George (Dalbuie)	35	27 March 1856 Single; farmer; brother of Alexander Donaldson; son of John Donaldson & Margaret Donaldson, ms Torrie	Ardclach Churchyard
DUNBAR, Isabella (Lethen Mills)	10	25 July 1857 Daughter of Rev Robert Dunbar, Free Church Minister, Pluscarden, & Jean Dunbar, ms Sutherland	Auldearn Churchyard
ELLIS, Elspet (Fornighty)	65	8 September 1860 Married; grandmother of John Cumming; daughter of John Collie & Elspet Collie, ms Duncan	Ardclach Churchyard
ELLIS, William	40	20 December 1860 Married; farmer; uncle of John Cumming; son of Alexander Collie & Elspet Collie, ms Collie	Ardclach Churchyard
FALCONER, James	13	15 May 1856 Nephew of Hugh Falconer; son of Alexander Falconer & Christian Fraser	Ardclach Churchyard
FALCONER, Janet	73	14 April 1857 Widow; mother of James Falconer; daughter of John Murdoch & Mary Murdoch, ms Mitchell	Ardclach Churchyard
FALCONER, Margaret (Blarley)	76	5 July 1855 Widow of Alexander Falconer; mother in law of James Donald; father of 5; daughter of Lachlan	Ardclach Churchyard
FALCONER, William	27	28 March 1855 Son of James Falconer & Jane Falconer, ms Murdoch Brother of James Falconer	Ardclach Churchyard

Name/Place of Death	Age	Date/Details	Burial Place
FRASER, Ann (Craigiemore)	3	14 May 1856 Daughter of John Fraser & Ann Fraser, ms Fraser	Auldearn Churchyard
FRASER, Christina (Wester Craigiemore)	21m	27 July 1857 Daughter of John Fraser & Ann Fraser, ms Fraser	Auldearn Churchyard
FRASER, Elizabeth	46	29 August 1859 Married; sister of Alexander Rose; daughter of Donald Rose & Jane Rose, ms Rose	Ardclach Churchyard
FRASER, Janet (Little Mill)	4	12 February 1858 Daughter of James Fraser & Margaret Fraser, ms McLennan	Ardclach Churchyard
FRASER, John (Wester Craigiemore)	62	20 January 1859 Married; farmer; son of William Fraser & Jane Fraser, ms Gowie	Auldearn Churchyard
FRASER, Mary (Little Mill)	60	5 August 1856 Single; daughter of Simon Fraser & Jane Fraser, ms Grant	Auldearn Churchyard
GLASS, Margaret	69	6 January 1856 Widow; mother of James Glass; daughter of James McQueen & Eliza Rose	Nairn Churchyard
GORDON, Mary	78	17 June 1860 Single; daughter of James Gordon & Jane Gordon, ms Stewart	Ardclach Churchyard
GRANT, Alexander (Berryburn)	10	24 May 1860 Son of Donald Grant & Jane Grant, ms Steele	Edinkillie Churchyard

Name/Place of Death	Age	Date/Details	Burial Place
GRANT, Mary (Little Culmoney)	6	6 November 1857 Daughter of John Grant & Janet Grant, ms McDonald	Ardclach Churchyard
HAY, William	73	30 January 1855 Labourer; father of 7; son of George Hay & Janet Hay, ms Watson	Ardclach Churchyard
KENNEDY, John (Leubrattoch)	79	13 June 1855 Widower of Ann Alexander; father of 6; including John; son of Malcolm Kennedy & Janet Kennedy, ms Kennedy	Ardclach Churchyard
KINNAIRD, Colin (Rumachroy)	17d	11 March 1856 Infant son of Colin Kinnaird & Margaret Kinnaird, ms Paterson	Cawdor Churchyard
LAWSON, William	75	2 May 1855 Husband of Janet McKenzie carpenter; son of Alexander Lawson & Jane Lawson, ms McKenzie	Auldearn
LESLIE, Jane (Drumlochan)	58	1 March 1858 Married; sister of Duncan Murdoch; daughter of John Murdoch & Mary Murdoch, ms Mitchell	Ardclach Churchyard
MACKINTOSH, Euan	71	17 May 1855 Married to Janet father of 5, including Finlay Mackintosh; son of Findlay Mackintosh & Helen Mackintosh, ms MacGillivray	Ardclach Churchyard
MCARTHUR, Ann (Newlands of Fleenas)	67	25 September 1858 Married; aunt of Alexander Kinnaird; daughter of James Kinnaird & Isabella, Kinnaird, ms Mackintosh	Ardclach Churchyard

Name/Place of Death	Age	Date/Details	Burial Place
MCBEAN, John	71	2 January 1857 Married; farmer; father of Peter McBean; son of Peter McBean & Catherine McBean, ms McLean	Geddes Burying Gr
MCDONALD, Alexander	82	30 December 1855 Husband of ? McIntyre; farmer; father of 7, including Peter McDonald; son of Donald McDonald & Catharine McDonald, ms Rose	Berivan
MCDONALD, Christina	70	18 February 1858 Married; mother of William Macdonald; daughter of John McQueen, schoolmaster, & Jane McQueen, ms Alexander	Ardclach Churchyard
MCDONALD, Ewan (Balanriech)	81	10 January 1858 Single; farmer; son of John McDonald & Elspet McDonald, ms MacKintosh	Ardclach Churchyard
MCDONALD, Isabella (Keppernach)	3	4 February 1857 Daughter of John McDonald & Elspet McDonald, ms MacKenzie	Ardclach Churchyard
MCDONALD, Isabella	84	6 May 1860 Widow; mother of Alexander McDonald; daughter of Alexander McBean & Ann McBean, ms McBeath	Ardclach Churchyard
MCDONALD, James (Achanruat)	35	1 April 1856 Single; schoolmaster; brother of Duncan Macdonald & Christina McDonald, ms McQueen	Ardclach Churchyard

Name/Place of Death	Age	Date/Details	Burial Place
MCDONALD, James	87	15 May 1856 Married; farmer; father of John McDonald; son of John McDonald alias Callum & Elspet McDonald, ms McKintosh	Ardclach Churchyard
MCDONALD, James (Keppernach)	9m	18 May 1858 Son of John McDonald & Elspet McDonald, ms MacKenzie	Ardclach Churchyard
MCDONALD, Jane	79	11 July 1855 Widow of Duncan McDonald; mother of Alexr McDonald; daughter of William Rose & Margaret Rose, ms McPherson	Ardclach Churchyard
MCDONALD, John (Tomnagee)	76	14 June 1856 Married; farmer; father of Thomas McDonald; son of John McDonald & Margaret McDonald, ms Fraser	Ch/yard of Inverness
MCDONALD, John (Belivat)	87	8 November 1857 Married; weaver; father of Hugh McDonald; son of Donald McDonald & Catherine McDonald, ms Ross	Ardclach Churchyard
MCDONALD, John	0	9 April 1860 Son of Donald McDonald & ? McDonald, ms Fraser	Ardclach Churchyard
MCGILLIVRAY, Alexander (Lubliester)	88	28 December 1859 Widower; mason; father of Hugh McGillivray; son of Alexander McGillivray & Margaret McGillivray, ms McHastie	Ardclach Churchyard

Name/Place of Death	Age	Date/Details	Burial Place
MCGILLIVRAY, Jessie (Dalnaheglish)	28	17 May 1857 Single; sister of David McGillivray; daughter of Alexander McGillivray & Harriet McGillivray, ms Rose	Ardclach Churchyard
MCGILLIVRAY, John	86	28 May 1857 Uncle of James Kennedy; son of John McGillvray & Ann McGillivray, ms McPherson	Ardclach Churchyard
MCGRIGOR, Mary (village of Ferness)	9m	1 February 1859 Daughter of James McGrigor & Margaret McGrigor, ms Jack	Ardclach Churchyard
MCINTOSH, Elspet (Wester Logie)	91	18 March 1860 Widow; daughter of John McIntosh & Helen McIntosh, ms McIntosh	Ardclach Churchyard
MCKAY, Alexander	37	15 September 1858 Single; lunatic; son of Donald McKay & Elspet McKay, ms Cumming	Ardclach Churchyard
MACKAY, Charlotte Penelope	13	23 November 1857 Daughter of John MacKay & Jane MacKay, ms Bain	Croy Churchyard
MCKAY, John	46	17 September 1857 Single; shoemaker; son of Donald McKay & Elspet McKay, ms Cumming	Ardclach Churchyard
MACKENZIE, Alexander (Keppernach)	32	31 January 1858 Single; tailor; brother in law of John McDonald; son of Alexander MacKenzie & Isabella MacKenzie, ms McLean	Cromdale Churchyard

Name/Place of Death	Age	Date/Details	Burial Place
MCKENZIE, Jane (Balnakiver)	77	25 June 1857 Wife of John McKenzie; daughter of David Rose & Ann Rose, ms Cameron	Cawdor Churchyard
MACKENZIE, Jane	76	2 July 1859 Single; daughter of Alexander MacKenzie & Mary MacKenzie, ms Cameron	Ardclach Churchyard
MCKILLICAN, Margaret (Achagour)	60	13 September 1857 Single; sister of John McKillican; daughter of William McKillican & Isabella McKillican, ms Mackintosh	Cawdor Churchyard
MACKINTOSH, Angus (Little Mill)	70	18 December 1860 Widower; labourer; son of Donald Mackintosh & Isabella Mackintosh, ms Mackintosh	Ardclach Churchyard
MACKINTOSH, Ann (Belivat)	76	22 July 1857 Widow; mother of John MacKintosh; daughter of John Falconer & Margaret Falconer, ms Clark	Ardclach Churchyard
MACKINTOSH, Ann	65	7 March 1858 Married; mother of William McIntosh; daughter of Alexander Campbell & Margaret Gilbert	Auldearn Churchyard
MACKINTOSH, Ann (Ferness Village)	34	12 February 1859 Wife of Hugh Mackintosh; daughter of James Forbes & Margaret Forbes, ms Mackintosh	Nairn Churchyard

Name/Place of Death	Age	Date/Details	Burial Place
MACKINTOSH, Betsey (Ferness Village)	10m	16 March 1859 Daughter of Hugh MacKintosh & Ann MacKintosh, ms Forbes	Nairn Churchyard
MACKINTOSH, Betsey	61	12 July 1860 Wife of James MacKintosh; daughter of Donald Fraser & Catherine Fraser, ms Rose	Ardclach Churchyard
MACKINTOSH, John (Easter Belivat)	46	16 August 1860 Married; farmer; brother of Allan MacKintosh; son of Robert MacKintosh & Ann MacKintosh, ms Falconer	Ardclach Churchyard
MACKINTOSH, James	75	19 November 1860 Widower; farmer; father of Alexr MacKintosh; son of James MacKintosh & Mary MacKintosh, ms Gowie	Ardclach Churchyard
MACKINTOSH, Margaret (Bridge of Logie)	43	20 October 1860 Single; sister of Allan MacKintosh; daughter of Robert MacKintosh & Ann MacKintosh, ms Falconer	Ardclach Churchyard
MCLEAN, Ann	16	2 November 1858 Daughter of Hector McLean & Ann McLean, ms McQueen	Ardclach Churchyard
MCLEAN, Margaret	70	27 May 1857 Widow; mother of Lachlan McLean; daughter of John Rose & Margaret Rose, ms Rose	Ardclach Churchyard
MCLEAN, William	77	19 September 1860 Married; labourer; father of Lachlan McLean; son of Alexander McLean & Janet McLean, ms McLean	Cawdor Churchyard

Name/Place of Death	Age	Date/Details	Burial Place
MCPHAIL, Margaret (Newlands of Fleenas)	68	17 February 1858 Widow; mother in law of James McIntosh; daughter of Peter Shaw & Isabella Shaw, ms Shaw	Ardclach Churchyard
MCPHERSON, Ann	4	6 October 1856 Dughter of James McPherson & Ann McPherson, ms McDonald	Ardclach Churchyar
MCPHERSON, Christina (Keppernach)	44	8 May 1860 Wife of John McPherson; daughter of John Kennedy & Ann Kennedy, ms Alexander	Ardclach Churchyard
MCPHERSON, Isabella (Balnuilt)	76	26 January 1860 Widow; mother in law of James Falconer; daughter of Alexander Fraser & Catherine Fraser, ms Mackintosh	Ardclach Churchyard
MCPHERSON, John (Easter Logie)	13	11 April 1858 Daughter of Donald McPherson & Margaret McPherson, ms Mackintosh	Ardclach Churchyard
MCPHERSON, John (Dulsie)	56	16 May 1859 Married; farm servant; son of James McPherson & Catherine McPherson, ms McPherson	Ardclach Churchyard
MCPHERSON, Margaret	61	4 March 1860 Single; daughter of William McPherson & Jane McPherson, ms Clark	Ardclach Churchyard
MCPHERSON, Thomas Stewart Brodie	20	31 March 1859 Single; son of Angus McPherson & Jane McPherson, ms McArthur	Cawdor Churchyard

Name/Place of Death	Age	Date/Details	Burial Place
MCQUEEN, James	73	17 August 1855 Father of William McQueen; son of John McQueen	Ardclach Churchyard
MCQUEEN, Jane (Bilivat)	80	23 November 1858 Widow; mother of Donald McQueen; daughter of Donald McQueen, army captain, & Janet Mackenzie	Ardclach Churchyard
MILNE, Catherine (Balmakiver)	9	5 March 1857 Daughter of Donald Milne & Helen Milne, ms McDonald	Ardclach Churchyard
NIGERTY, Elizabeth	2	7 December 1857 Daughter of George Nigerty & Mary Nigerty, ms McDonald	Ardclach Churchyard
RALPH, Alexander	67	2 April 1855 Son of Alexander Ralph	Dyke Churchyard
ROBERTSON, Alexander (Keppernach)	65	8 April 1856 Single; farmer; brother of James Robertson; son of John Robertson & Anna Robertson, ms Mackintosh	Auldearn Churchyard
ROSE, Donald	41	4 June 1858 Married; carpenter; brother of Alex Rose; son of Alexander Rose & Catherine Rose, ms Rose	Geddes Burying Gr
ROSE, Donald	77	10 August 1858 Married; farmer; father of Alexander Rose; son of Alexander Rose & Elizabeth Rose, ms Falconer	Ardclach Churchyard
ROSE, James	75	8 November 1858 Single; farmer; son of David Rose & Ann Rose, ms Cameron	Ardclach Churchyard

Name/Place of Death	Age	Date/Details	Burial Place
ROSE, Jane (Little Mill)	64	19 January 1858 Married; daughter of John Rose & Elizabeth Rose, ms Rose	Ardclach Churchyard
ROSE, Jane	77	23 February 1860 Widow; mother of Alexander Rose; daughter of Alexander Rose & Harriet Rose, ms McAndrew	Ardclach Churchyard
ROSE, William	83	10 February 1858 Widower; pensioner; brother in law of John Ross; son of William Rose & Janet Rose, ms Mackintosh	Ardclach Churchyard
ROSS, Amelia (Balnacraig)	68	13 November 1858 Wife of Charles Ross; daughter of Alexander Fraser & Ann Fraser, ms Fraser	Ardclach Churchyard
SIMPSON, Jane (Mill of Airdrie)	82	9 February 1858 Married; daughter of William Ross & Helen Ross, ms Simpson	Edinkillie Churchyard
SMITH, James	86	17 October 1857 Single; farmer; son of Francis Smith & Janet Smith, ms Grant	Ardclach Churchyard
ROSS, James	57	1 April 1859 Single, labourer; son of William Ross & Helen Ross, ms Simpson	Edinkillie Churchyard
STEWART, Mary	89	8 December 1856 Widow; grandmother of Alexr McDonald; daughter of Alexander Robertson & Jane Robertson, ms Fraser	Auldearn Churchyard

Name/Place of Death	Age	Date/Details	Burial Place
WATT, Hector McLean (Banchar)	7	10 March 1858 Son of Donald Watt & Jess Watt, ms McLean	Ardclach Churchyard

The Parishes of Nairnshire
Deaths & Burial Places
1855-1860

Cawdor Parish

Name/Place of Death	Age	Date/Details	Burial Place
BENZIE, Margaret (Brackla)	47	18 June 1858 Married to James Benzie; Daur of James Brodie & Jane Brodie, ms Stephenson	Cawdor Churchyard
BRYCE, Margaret (Inchornie)	63	20 March 1857 Wife of John Bryce; daughter of William Guthrie & Margaret Guthrie, ms Thornton	Cawdor Churchyard
CAMERON, female	4d	30 May 1857 Daur of Donald Cameron, Farmer, & Mary Grant, house servant	Bairievan Burial Gr
CAMERON, Alexander (Dalcharn)	19	4 November 1859 Single; Draper's Assistant; Son of Alexander Cameron & Jane Mackenzie	Daviot Churchyard
CAMERON, Flora	13	23 December 1855 Daur of John Cameron & Sarah McDonald	Ardersier Burial Gr
CAMPBELL, John	73	13 February 1856 Chelsea Pensioner; married; Son of John Campbell & Janet Campbell, ms Cameron	Cawdor Churchyard
CLARK, Alexander (Newlands of Torrich)	82	10 February 1859 Married; father of Catherine Anderson; son of John Clark & Bell Macpherson	Cawdor Churchyard
CLARK, Margaret Jane	26d	5 November 1856 Infant daur of John Clark & Christina Clark, ms Munro	Cawdor Churchyard
CLARK, Margaret (Newton of Budgate)	27	19 May 1859 Single; sister of Mary Clark; daughter of William Clark & Janet Clark, ms Munro	Cawdor Churchyard

Name/Place of Death	Age	Date/Details	Burial Place
DALLAS, Alexander (Inchyettle)	25d	12 August 1859 Inf son of Duncan Dallas & Ann Falconer	Barievain Churchyard
DAVIDSON, Isabella (Welltown)	79	10 February 1858 Widow, pauper; grandmother of John Falconer; daughter of John Davidson & Margaret Davidson, ms Mackintosh	Cawdor Churchyard
DUNCAN, Peter (Milton of Cawdor)	88	4 March 1860 Pauper, formerly farmer; widower; parents unknown by informant	Cawdor Churchyars
ELLIS, Elspet	56	18 May 1857 Wife of James Ellis, labourer; daughter of James McKenzie & Ann McKenzie, ms Falconer	Cawdor Churchyard
FALCONER, Margaret (Rineach)	63	8 August 1859 Wife of William Falconer; daughter of Peter McArthur & Isabella Rose	Cawdor Churchyard
FALCONER, May (Fleachy Moss)	14	30 July 1858 Single; daughter of Donald Falconer & Jane Falconer, ms Macpherson	Cawdor Churchyard
FINDLATER, Henrietta (Newlands of Broomhill)	c75	26 February 1860 Single; pauper; parents unknown to informant	Cawdor Churchyard
FRASER, male (Standalone)	1h	30 September 1860 Infant son of Alexr Fraser & Margaret Fraser, ms Ogilvie	Cawdor Churchyard
FRASER, Alexander (Cawdor)	4	15 April 1858 Son of Alexander Fraser & Mary Fraser, ms Urquhart	Cawdor Churchyard

Name/Place of Death	Age	Date/Details	Burial Place
FRASER, Ann	69	15 January 1858 Widow; pauper; mother of Alexr Fraser; daughter of Duncan Campbell & Ann Edom	Cawdor Churchyard
FRASER, Catherine (Newlands of Clunas)	70	3 April 1860 Single; pauper; sister of Alexr Fraser, Auldearn; daughter of Alexr Fraser & Rebecca McIntosh	Cawdor Churchyard
FRASER, Donald (Dallaschoile)	59	27 November 1860 Husband of Ann; pauper, formerly ag lab; son of Hugh Fraser & Elizabeth Fraser, ms Ross	Croy Churchyard
FRASER, Elizabeth Mary	5	23 February 1855 Daughter of Robert Fraser & Mary Forbes Fraser, ms Gordon	Cawdor Churchyard
FRASER, Jemima	5	26 August 1855 Daughter of John Fraser & Mary Fraser, ms McKenzie (decd)	Cawdor Churchyard
FRASER, Margaret (Newlands of Clunas)	84	23 April 1860 Pauper; widow; mother in law of Robert McIntosh; daughter of Donald Mackenzie & Kate Davidson	Cawdor Churchyard
FRASER, Martha (Cawdor)	90	21 August 1858 Schoolmaster's widow; parents n/k to informant	Kirkyard of Bereven
FRASER, Mary (Drumurinie)	53	5 September 1860 Widow; mother of James Fraser; daughter of Donald Forbes & Mary Forbes, ms Fraser	Boleskine Churchyard

Name/Place of Death	Age	Date/Details	Burial Place
FRASER, Thomas (Drumurinie)	62	18 May 1860 Married; farmer; father of Simon Fraser; son of Simon Fraser & Margt McIntosh	Boleskine Burial Gr
GOWANS, Christina (Newton of Budgate)	18h	30 July 1859 Daughter of Charles Gowans & Catharine Sharp; granddaughter of James Sharp	Cawdor Churchyard
GRANT, Alexander (Inchsettle)	85	17 April 1857 Widower; father of Alexander Grant; son of Alexander Grant & Ann Grant, ms Davidson	Cawdor Churchyard
GRANT, Isabella (Blairmore)	70	7 October 1859 Widow; aunt of David Tulloch; daughter of John Tulloch & Ann Eddie	Cawdor Churchyard
GRANT, Margaret (Inchsettle)	62	9 July 1860 Single; field worker; sister of Alexr Grant; daughter of Alexander Grant & Ann McDonald	Cawdor Churchyard
HENDRY, James (Auchneem)	74	21 November 1860 Widower; farmer; father of Simon Hendry; son of William Hendry & Helen	Auldearn Churchyard
KEY, George (Dallaschoile)	17d	17 January 1860 Infant son of Ebenezer Key & Rose Wilson	Cawdor Churchyard
LAWSON, William	c 40	31 December 1855 Accidental Drowning; parents n/k to Informant	Cawdor Churchyard
MASON, William (Newlands of Cawdor)	20	11 January 1855 Son of David Mason & Ann Mason, ms McDonald	Cawdor Churchyard

Name/Place of Death	Age	Date/Details	Burial Place
MASSON, David	14	8 May 1857 Son of David Masson & Ann Masson, ms McDonald	Cawdor Churchyard
MASSON, William (Newlands of Clunas)	59	16 April 1859 Married; father of William Masson; son of John Masson & Ann Masson, ms Fraser	Barievain Churchyard
MCARTHUR, Ann	80	12 July 1857 Widow; pauper; mother of Duncan Fraser; daughter of Duncan McArthur	Cawdor Churchyard
MCBEAN, William (Dalcharn)	38	29 November 1858 Single, Cattle Dealer; brother of Alexr McBean; son of John McBean & May McBean, ms Rose	Dunlichity Ch/yard
MCDONALD, Ann (Blairmore)	39	26 July 1856 Married to Alexander McDonald; daughter of Alexander Rose & Grace Rose, ms McIntyre	Cawdor Churchyard
MCDONALD, Donald	73	25 April 1855 Married to Janet McDonald, ms Mackintosh	Cawdor Churchyard
MACDONALD, Donald (Newlands of Urchany)	70	12 September 1858 Married to Ann; son of Alexander Macdonald & Mary Macdonald, ms Urquhart	Cawdor Churchyard
MACDONALD, James (Knockard)	9m	18 April 1858 Son of James Macdonald & Ann Fraser	Cawdor Churchyard
MCGILLIVRAY, David	30	6 March 1857 Widower; Chelsea Pensioner; son of John McGillivray & Mary McGillivray, ms Ross	Cawdor Churchyard

Name/Place of Death	Age	Date/Details	Burial Place
MCGILLIVRAY, Jane (Standalone)	22	18 June 1857 Single; daughter of Donald McGillivray & Kate McGillivray, ms Macdonald	Cawdor Churchyard
MCGILLIVRAY, Margaret (Raitknock)	80	31 August 1860 Widow; pauper; mother of Jane McGillivray; daughter of Donald Campbell & Jane Campbell, ms Cameron	Geddes Churchyard
MCGRIGOR, Donald	85	21 June 1856 Widower, hand-loom weaver; parents n/k to informant; father of Donald McGrigor	Cawdor Churchyard
MCGRIGOR, Ewen	13m	16 September 1857 Daughter of Ann McGrigor; ag lab	Croy Churchyard
MCINTOSH, Janet (Drynichan)	74	8 March 1858 Miller's widow; mother of William McIntosh; daughter of William Morrison & Janet Morrison, ms Mackay	Moy-Hall Churchyard
MCINTYRE, John	79	17 December 1858 Single; uncle of Henrietta Rose; son of Peter McIntyre & Christian McIntyre, ms Johnston	Cawdor Churchyard
MCKAY, Bessie (Baluarait)	86	7 February 1860 Pauper; wife of David McKay; daughter of Peter McIntyre & Chirsty Johnstone	Croy Churchyard
MACKENZIE, David	15m	11 August 1857 Son of Francis Mackenzie, Chelsea Pensioner, & Jessie Mackenzie, ms Masson	Cawdor Churchyard

Name/Place of Death	Age	Date/Details	Burial Place
MACKENZIE, Donald	16	11 July 1857 Single, farm servant of Campbell Smith; son of Roderick Mackenzie & ? Mackenzie, ms Finlayson	Geddes Burial Gr
MCKENZIE, Elizabeth	56	12 November 1855 Married; daughter of Alexander McKenzie & Ann McKenzie, ms McKenzie Mother of 6 children	Cawdor Churchyard
MCKENZIE, Francis	23	10 April 1855 Son of Francis McKenzie & Janet McKenzie, ms Mason	Cawdor Churchyard
MACKENZIE, Hector (Whinhill)	80	2 February 1858 Widower; cooper; father of Jean Mackenzie; son of William Mackenzie & May Mackenzie, ms Young	Cawdor Churchyard
MACKENZIE, James (Broomhill)	63	2 September 1858 Married; mason's labourer; father of Charles Mackenzie; son of Donald Mackenzie & Ann Mackenzie, ms Clark	Petty Churchyard
MCKENZIE, Janet	38	29 December 1856 Single, cook domestic; daughter of Roderick McKenzie & Margaret McKenzie, ms McGlashan; brother of Roderick McKenzie	Cawdor Churchyard
MACKENZIE, Janet (Newlands of Torrich)	80	13 November 1858 Single; pauper; aunt of Catherine Anderson; daughter of Andrew Mackenzie & Eppie Mackenzie, ms McKillican	Cawdor Churchyard

Name/Place of Death	Age	Date/Details	Burial Place
MACKENZIE, Margaret (Village of Cawdor)	42	5 June 1859 Husband of Roderick Mackenzie; daughter of Donald Macdonald & Ann Macdonald, ms Mackintosh	Cawdor Churchyard
MCKENZIE, Sophia (Balintore)	67	8 July 1859 Pauper; mason's widow; mother of Margaret; daughter of John McLean & Isabella Macdonald	Cawdor Churchyard
MACKENZIE, William	18	17 July 1857 Single; farm servant of Campbell Smith; son of Roderick Mackenzie & ? Mackenzie, ms Finlayson	Geddes Burial Gr
MACKENZIE, William	57	8 November 1857 Married; mason; father of Margaret; son of John Mackenzie & Margaret Mackenzie, ms Rose	Cawdor Churchyard
MACKILLICAN, Thomas	92	14 July 1855 Married to 1) Bell McIntyre & 2) Elizabeth Gordon; father of 4; including James MacKillican; son of Thomas MacKillican & Janet MacKillican, ms Finlayson	Cawdor Churchyard
MACKINTOSH, Elizabeth (Doghill)	75	27 July 1860 Single; pauper; sister of William Mackintosh; daughter of John Mackintosh & Elizabeth Mackintosh, ms Rose	Braeclach Burial Gr
MACKINTOSH, Isabella (Doghill)	79	1 February 1858 Single; pauper; daughter of John Mackintosh & Elizabeth Mackintosh, ms Rose; sister of William	Braeclach Burial Gr

Name/Place of Death	Age	Date/Details	Burial Place
MACKINTOSH, Janet (Newlands of Piperhill)	89	1 February 1857 Widow; pauper; daughter of William McDonald	Cawdor Churchyard
MACKINTOSH, Janet (Newlands of Clunas)	110	23 January 1858 Widow; pauper; mother of John Mackintosh; daughter of John Macdonald	Cawdor Churchyard
MACKINTOSH, Janet (Auchindoun)	60	3 December 1858 Widow; ag lab; sister of Isabella Ross; daughter of William Ross & Janet Ross, ms MacArthur	Croy Churchyard
MACKINTOSH, Margaret (Doghill)	74	21 May 1858 Single; pauper; daughter of John Mackintosh & Elizabeth Mackintosh, ms Rose; sister of William Mackintosh	Braeclach Burial Gr
MACKINTOSH, Margaret (Dallaschoile)	87	15 October 1858 Pauper; mother of Marjory Marjory Mackintosh; daughter of John Mackintosh & Marjory Mackintosh, ms MacLean	Croy Churchyard
MACLEOD, John	14m	25 November 1857 Son of John MacLeod & Isabella MacLeod, ms MacVicar	Cawdor Churchyard
MCNISHIE, Anabella	62	27 March 1856 Pauper; single; parents n/k to informant	Cawdor Churchyard
MACPHERSON, Isabella	34	1 December 1860 Single; sister of John Macpherson; daur of Lachlan Macpherson & Madlina Macpherson, ms Macpherson	Cawdor Churchyard

Name/Place of Death	Age	Date/Details	Burial Place
MCPHERSON, Jean	23	9 April 1855 Single; daughter of James McPherson & Mary McPherson, ms Clark	Cawdor Churchyard
MCQUEEN, Isabella	77	1 July 1855 Widow of James McQueen; mother of Alexander	Moy Bhig Burial Gr
MCQUEEN, May or Mary	6	21 March 1857 Daughter of Alexander McQueen & May McQueen, ms McBain	Churchyard of Moy
MCTAVISH, James Dean (Dallaschoile)	7wk	8 December 1859 Infant son of Donald McTavish & Mary Mackintosh	Cawdor Churchyard
MASSON, John (Cawdor Mills)	75	24 March 1857 Single;.uncle of Alexander Sinclair; son of David Masson & Mary Robertson	Dyke Churchyard
MASSON, William (Newlands of Clunas)	59	16 April 1859 Married; father of William Masson; son of John Masson, shoemaker, & Ann Fraser	Barievain Churchyard
MORRISON, Alexander (Newlands of Broomhill)	75	2 September 1858 Married; crofter; father of John Morrison; son of Donald Morrison & Margaret Morrison, ms Macrae	Cawdor Churchyard
MUNRO, Esther (Newlands of Budgate)	82	19 April 1858 Widow; mother of Christina Ellis; daughter of Alexander Cameron & Catherine Cameron, ms Fraser	Cawdor Churchyard

Name/Place of Death	Age	Date/Details	Burial Place
MUNRO, John (Newlands of Broomhill)	25	22 October 1860 Single; day labourer; son of Donald Munro & Jean Reid (pauper)	Cawdor Churchyard
MURRAY, Robert (Buchrain Carrach)	8m	4 May 1859 Son of John Murray & Isabella Murray, ms Rose	Cawdor Churchyard
REID, Mary (Newlands of Piperhill)	84	21 January 1860 Single; Pauper, formerly domestic servant; daughter of Alexr Reid & Mary Reid, ms unknown	Cawdor Churchyard
ROBERTSON, Christina (Glengoullie)	86	21 March 1858 Shoemaker's widow; daughter of Donald Ross & Janet Ross, ms Ross; sister Isabella McPherson	Cawdor Churchyard
ROSE, Alexander	79	12 December 1856 Married; shoemaker; son of Hugh Rose & Henrietta McIlvane	Cawdor Churchyard
ROSE, John	76	1 January 1859 Married; shoemaker; father of John Ross; son of Alexander Rose & Mary Rose	Cawdor Churchyard
ROSE, John	c69	13 November 1859 Single; ag lab; brother of Isabella McIntosh; son of John Rose & Marsley Sinclair	Croy Churchyard
ROSS, Hugh	34	23 July 1856 Married; lawyer's clerk; son of Angus Ross & Ann Ross, ms Campbell; brother of Alexander Ross	Auldearn Churchyard

Name/Place of Death	Age	Date/Details	Burial Place
ROSS, William (Innis-nan-caorach)	78	22 October 1858 Widower; ag lab; parents n/k to informant	Nairn Churchyard
SCOTT, female (Polwark)	10min	28 January 1857 Son of James Scott & Agnes Scott, ms Allan	Cawdor Churchyard
SINCLAIR, William (Foxmoss)	56	9 February 1857 Married; father of Donald Sinclair; son of William Sinclair & Margaret Sinclair, ms Clunas	Cawdor Churchyard
SMITH, Christina (Dallaschoile)	57	22 November 1859 Widow of John Smith, (road contractor); sister of Elspet McIntosh; daughter of Alexander McIntosh & Margaret McIntosh	Daviot Churchyard
SMITH, Isabella (Raitloan)	41	24 March 1855 Married to Campbell Smith	Auldearn Churchyard
SMITH, John	81	10 June 1857 Married; road contractor; father of Alex Smith; son of William Smith & Christina Smith, ms Forbes	Daviot Churchyard
SOUTHERN, Ann (Polneach)	20	17 November 1859 Wife of Thomas Southern; daughter of John Findlay & Mary Skillington	Alves Ch/yrd (Moray)
STEEL, Jane	83	14 February 1856 Pauper; widow; daughter of John Falconer & Christina Mackintosh	Cawdor Churchyard

Name/Place of Death	Age	Date/Details	Burial Place
STEWART, Alexander	76	17 January 1858 Cartwright; widower; father of Margt McKenzie; son of John Stewart & Ann Stewart, ms Macpherson	Cawdor Churchyard
STEWART, Margaret (Cawdor)	79	24 September 1858 Single; pauper; aunt of Elspet MacIntosh; daughter of John Stewart, Miller, & Ann Stewart, ms Macpherson	Cawdor Churchyard
STEWART, William	7	24 August 1855 Son of Paul Stewart & Janet Stewart, ms Davidson	Cawdor Churchyard
STUART, Alexander (Newton of Budgate)	1d	8 December 1859 Son of Alexander Stuart & Ann Small	Cawdor Churchyard
TULLOCH, Barbara	80	2 October 1857 Crofter's widow; daughter of William Finlayson & Janet Finlayson, ms Macbean; mother in law of Duncan McKenzie	Cawdor Churchyard
TULLOCH, Margaret	37	6 April 1855 Single; daughter of Charles Tulloch & Isabella Tulloch, ms Davidson; sister in law of John Falconer	Cawdor Churchyard
SUPPOSED MENDICANT (Barn of Budgate)	c70	9 March 1857	Cawdor Churchyard

ISBN 978-0-9561937-2-8

Published by J & B Bishop for
Moray & Nairn FHS